Lamia

$4|50.

Dear Susie

From
Ida

Dec. 25 – 1888

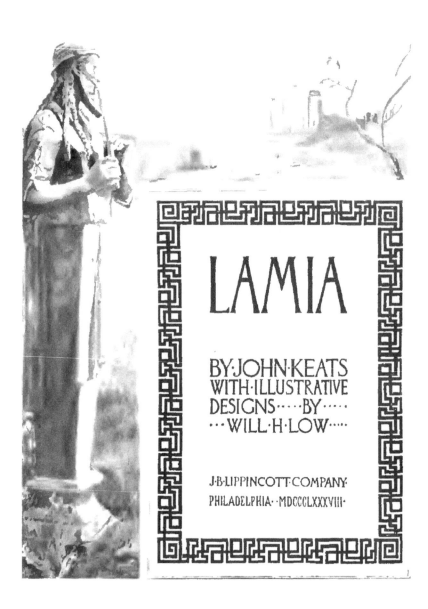

LAMIA

BY·JOHN·KEATS
WITH·ILLUSTRATIVE
DESIGNS·····BY·····
···WILL·H·LOW·····

J·B·LIPPINCOTT·COMPANY·
PHILADELPHIA·MDCCCLXXXVIII·

IN TESTIMONY OF LOYAL FRIEND
SHIP AND OF A COMMON FAITH IN
DOVBTFVL TALES FROM FAERY LAND
I DEDICATE TO
ROBERT LOVIS STEVENSON

Upon a time, before the faery broods

Drove Nymph and Satyr from the prosperous woods,

Before King Oberon's bright diadem,

Sceptre, and mantle, clasp'd with dewy gem,

Frighted away the Dryads and the Fauns

From rushes green, and brakes, and cowslipp'd lawns,

The ever-smitten Hermes empty left

His golden throne, bent warm on amorous theft:

From high Olympus had he stolen light,
On this side of Jove's clouds, to escape the sight
Of his great summoner, and made retreat
Into a forest on the shores of Crete
For somewhere in that sacred island dwelt
A nymph, to whom all hoofed Satyrs knelt;
At whose white feet the languid Tritons pour'd
Pearls, while on land they wither'd and adored.
Fast by the springs where she to bathe was wont,
And in those meads where sometime she might haunt,
Were strewn rich gifts, unknown to any Muse,
Though Fancy's casket were unlock'd to choose.
Ah, what a world of love was at her feet!
So Hermes thought, and a celestial heat
Burnt from his winged heels to either ear,
That from a whiteness, as the lily clear,
Blush'd into roses 'mid his golden hair,
Fallen in jealous curls about his shoulders bare.
From vale to vale, from wood to wood, he flew,
Breathing upon the flowers his passion new,
And wound with many a river to its head,
To find where this sweet nymph prepared her secret bed:

.

In vain; the sweet nymph might nowhere be found,
And so he rested, on the lonely ground,
Pensive, and full of painful jealousies
Of the Wood-Gods, and even the very trees.

There as he stood, he heard a mournful voice,
Such as once heard, in gentle heart, destroys
All pain but pity: thus the lone voice spake:
"When from this wreathed tomb shall I awake!
When move in a sweet body fit for life,
And love, and pleasure, and the ruddy strife
Of hearts and lips!   Ah, miserable me!"
The God, dove-footed, glided silently

Round bush and tree, soft-brushing, in his speed,
The taller grasses and full-flowering weed,
Until he found a palpitating snake,
Bright, and cirque-couchant in a dusky brake.

She was a gordian shape of dazzling hue,
Vermilion-spotted, golden, green, and blue ,
Striped like a zebra, freckled like a pard,
Eyed like a peacock, and all crimson barr'd
And full of silver moons, that, as she breathed,
Dissolved, or brighter shone, or interwreathed
Their lustres with the gloomier tapestries—
So rainbow-sided, touch'd with miseries,
She seem'd, at once, some penanced lady elf,
Some demon's mistress, or the demon's self.
Upon her crest she wore a wannish fire
Sprinkled with stars, like Ariadne's tiar :
Her head was serpent, but ah, bitter-sweet !
She had a woman's mouth with all its pearls complete :
And for her eyes—what could such eyes do there
But weep, and weep, that they were born so fair ?
As Proserpine still weeps for her Sicilian air

Her throat was serpent, but the words she spake
Came, as through bubbling honey, for Love's sake,
And thus; while Hermes on his pinions lay,
Like a stoop'd falcon ere he takes his prey:

"Fair Hermes! crown'd with feathers, fluttering light,
I had a splendid dream of thee last night;
I saw thee sitting, on a throne of gold,
Among the Gods, upon Olympus old,
The only sad one; for thou didst not hear
The soft, lute-finger'd Muses chanting clear,
Nor even Apollo when he sang alone,
Deaf to his throbbing throat's long, long melodious moan.

I dreamt I saw thee, robed in purple flakes,
Break amorous through the clouds, as morning breaks,
And, swiftly as a bright Phœbean dart,
Strike for the Cretan isle; and here thou art!
Too gentle Hermes, hast thou found the maid?"
Whereat the star of Lethe not delay'd
His rosy eloquence, and thus inquired:
"Thou smooth-lipp'd serpent, surely high-inspired!
Thou beauteous wreath, with melancholy eyes,
Possess whatever bliss thou canst devise,
Telling me only where my nymph is fled,—
Where she doth breathe!" "Bright planet, thou hast said,'
Return'd the snake, "but seal with oaths, fair God!"
"I swear," said Hermes, "by my serpent rod,
And by thine eyes, and by thy starry crown!"
Light flew his earnest words, among the blossoms blown.

Then thus again the brilliance feminine:
"Too frail of heart! for this lost nymph of thine,
Free as the air, invisibly, she strays
About these thornless wilds; her pleasant days
She tastes unseen; unseen her nimble feet
Leave traces in the grass and flowers sweet:

From weary tendrils, and bow'd branches green,
She plucks the fruit unseen, she bathes unseen:
And by my power is her beauty veil'd
To keep it unaffronted, unassail'd
By the love-glances of unlovely eyes,
Of Satyrs, Fauns, and blear'd Silenus' sighs.

Pale grew her immortality, for woe
Of all these lovers, and she grieved so
I took compassion on her, bade her steep
Her hair in weïrd syrops, that would keep
Her loveliness invisible, yet free
To wander as she loves, in liberty.
Thou shalt behold her, Hermes, thou alone,
If thou wilt, as thou swearest, grant my boon!"
Then, once again, the charmed God began
An oath, and through the serpent's ears it ran
Warm, tremulous, devout, psalterian.

Ravish'd she lifted her Circean head,
Blush'd a live damask, and swift-lisping said,
"I was a woman, let me have once more
A woman's shape, and charming as before.
I love a youth of Corinth—O the bliss!
Give me my woman's form, and place me where he is.
Stoop, Hermes, let me breathe upon thy brow,
And thou shalt see thy sweet nymph even now."

The God on half-shut feathers sank serene,
She breathed upon his eyes, and swift was seen
Of both the guarded nymph near-smiling on the green
It was no dream, or say a dream it was,
Real are the dreams of Gods, and smoothly pass
Their pleasures in a long immortal dream
One warm, flush'd moment, hovering, it might seem
Dash'd by the wood-nymph's beauty, so he burn'd,
Then, lighting on the printless verdure, turn'd
To the swoon'd serpent, and with languid arm,
Delicate, put to proof the lithe Caducean charm
So done, upon the nymph his eyes he bent
Full of adoring tears and blandishment,
And towards her stept· she, like a moon in wane,
Faded before him, cower'd, nor could restrain
Her fearful sobs, self-folding like a flower
That faints into itself at evening hour
But the God fostering her chilled hand,
She felt the warmth, her eyelids open'd bland,
And, like new flowers at morning song of bees,
Bloom'd, and gave up her honey to the lees
Into the green-recessed woods they flew,
Nor grew they pale, as mortal lovers do

Left to herself, the serpent now began
To change, her elfin blood in madness ran,
Her mouth foam'd, and the grass, therewith besprent,
Wither'd at dew so sweet and virulent;
Her eyes in torture fix'd, and anguish drear,
Hot, glazed, and wide, with lid-lashes all sear,
Flash'd phosphor and sharp sparks, without one cooling tear
The colors all inflamed throughout her train,
She writhed about, convulsed with scarlet pain ·
A deep volcanian yellow took the place
Of all her milder-mooned body's grace,
And, as the lava ravishes the mead,
Spoilt all her silver mail, and golden brede,
Made gloom of all her frecklings, streaks and bars,
Eclipsed her crescents and lick'd up her stars
So that, in moments few, she was undrest
Of all her sapphires, greens, and amethyst,
And rubious-argent of all these bereft
Nothing but pain and ugliness were left.
Still shone her crown, that vanish'd, also she
Melted and disappear'd as suddenly
And in the air, her new voice luting soft,

25

Cried, "Lycius! gentle Lycius!"—Borne aloft
With the bright mists about the mountains hoar
These words dissolved: Crete's forests heard no more.

 Whither fled Lamia, now a lady bright,
A full-born beauty new and exquisite?
She fled into that valley they pass o'er
Who go to Corinth from Cenchreas' shore;
And rested at the foot of those wild hills,
The rugged founts of the Peræan rills,
And of that other ridge whose barren back
Stretches, with all its mist and cloudy rack,
South-westward to Cleone. There she stood
About a young bird's flutter from a wood,
Fair, on a sloping green of mossy tread,
By a clear pool, wherein she passioned
To see herself escaped from so sore ills,
While her robes flaunted with the daffodils.

Ah ! happy Lycius !—for she was a maid
More beautiful than ever twisted braid,
Or sigh'd, or blush'd, or on spring-flower'd lea
Spread a green kirtle to the minstrelsy
A virgin purest lipp'd, yet in the lore
Of love deep learned to the red heart's core
Not one hour old, yet of sciential brain
To unperplex bliss from its neighbor pain ,
Define their pettish limits, and estrange
Their points of contact, and swift counterchange ,
Intrigue with the specious chaos, and dispart
Its most ambiguous atoms with sure art :
As though in Cupid's college she had spent
Sweet days a lovely graduate, still unshent,
And kept his rosy terms in idle languishment.

Why this fair creature chose so faerily
By the wayside to linger, we shall see ,
But first tis fit to tell how she could muse
And dream, when in the serpent prison-house,
Of all she list, strange or magnificent ·
How, ever, where she will'd, her spirit went ,

Whether to faint Elysium, or where
Down through tress-lifting waves the Nereids fair
Wind into Thetis' bower by many a pearly stair;
Or where God Bacchus drains his cups divine,
Stretch'd out, at ease, beneath a glutinous pine;
Or where in Pluto's gardens palatine
Mulciber's columns gleam in far piazzian line.
And sometimes into cities she would send
Her dream, with feast and rioting to blend;
And once, while among mortals dreaming thus,
She saw the young Corinthian Lycius
Charioting foremost in the envious race,
Like a young Jove with calm uneager face.

And fell into a swooning love of him
Now on the moth-time of that evening dim
He would return that way, as well she knew,
To Corinth from the shore, for freshly blew
The eastern soft wind, and his galley now
Grated the quay-stones with her brazen prow
In port Cenchreas, from Egina isle
Fresh anchor'd, whither he had been awhile
To sacrifice to Jove, whose temple there
Waits with high marble doors for blood and incense rare
Jove heard his vows, and better'd his desire;
For by some freakful chance he made retire
From his companions, and set forth to walk.
Perhaps grown wearied of their Corinth talk,
Over the solitary hills he fared,
Thoughtless, at first, but ere eve's star appear'd
His phantasy was lost, where reason fades,
In the calm'd twilight of Platonic shades
Lamia beheld him coming, near, more near—
Close to her passing, in indifference drear
His silent sandals swept the mossy green,
So neighbor'd to him, and yet so unseen

She stood: he pass'd, shut up in mysteries,
His mind wrapp'd like his mantle, while her eyes
Follow'd his steps, and her neck regal white
Turn'd—syllabling thus, "Ah, Lycius bright!
And will you leave me on the hills alone?
Lycius, look back! and be some pity shown."
He did; not with cold wonder fearingly,
But Orpheus-like at an Eurydice;
For so delicious were the words she sung,
It seem'd he had loved them a whole summer long:

And soon his eyes had drunk her beauty up,
Leaving no drop in the bewildering cup,
And still the cup was full,—while he, afraid
Lest she should vanish ere his lip had paid
Due adoration, thus began to adore,
Her soft look growing coy, she saw his chain so sure:
"Leave thee alone! Look back! Ah, Goddess, see
Whether my eyes can ever turn from thee!
For pity do not this sad heart belie—
Even as thou vanishest so I shall die
Stay! though a Naiad of the rivers, stay!
To thy far wishes will thy streams obey
Stay! though the greenest woods be thy domain,
Alone they can drink up the morning rain,
Though a descended Pleiad, will not one
Of thine harmonious sisters keep in tune
Thy spheres, and as thy silver proxy shine?
So sweetly to these ravish'd ears of mine
Came thy sweet greeting, that if thou shouldst fade
Thy memory will waste me to a shade —
For pity do not melt!"—"If I should stay,"
Said Lamia, "here, upon this floor of clay,

And pain my steps upon these flowers too rough,
What canst thou say or do of charm enough
To dull the nice remembrance of my home?
Thou canst not ask me with thee here to roam
Over these hills and vales, where no joy is,—
Empty of immortality and bliss!
Thou art a scholar, Lycius, and must know
That finer spirits cannot breathe below
In human climes, and live. Alas! poor youth,
What taste of purer air hast thou to soothe
My essence? What serener palaces,
Where I may all my many senses please,
And by mysterious sleights a hundred thirsts appease?
It cannot be—Adieu!" So said, she rose
Tiptoe with white arms spread He, sick to lose
The amorous promise of her lone complain,
Swoon'd, murmuring of love, and pale with pain.
The cruel lady, without any show
Of sorrow for her tender favorite's woe,
But rather, if her eyes could brighter be,
With brighter eyes and slow amenity,
Put her new lips to his, and gave afresh

The life she had so tangled in her mesh
And as he from one trance was wakening
Into another, she began to sing,
Happy in beauty, life, and love, and everything,
A song of love, too sweet for earthly lyres,
While, like held breath, the stars drew in their panting fires
And then she whisper'd in such trembling tone,
As those who, safe together met alone
For the first time through many anguish'd days,
Use other speech than looks, bidding him raise
His drooping head, and clear his soul of doubt,
For that she was a woman, and without
Any more subtle fluid in her veins
Than throbbing blood, and that the self-same pains
Inhabited her frail-strung heart as his
And next she wonder'd how his eyes could miss
Her face so long in Corinth, where, she said,
She dwelt but half retired, and there had led
Days happy as the gold coin could invent
Without the aid of love; yet in content
Till she saw him, as once she pass'd him by,
Where 'gainst a column he leant thoughtfully

37

At Venus' temple porch, 'mid baskets heap'd
Of amorous herbs and flowers, newly reap'd
Late on that eve, as 'twas the night before
The Adonian feast; whereof she saw no more,
But wept alone those days, for why should she adore?
Lycius from death awoke into amaze,
To see her still, and singing so sweet lays;
Then from amaze into delight he fell
To hear her whisper woman's lore so well;
And every word she spake enticed him on
To unperplex'd delight and pleasure known
Let the mad poets say whate'er they please
Of the sweets of Faeries, Peris, Goddesses,
There is not such a treat among them all,
Haunters of cavern, lake, and waterfall,
As a real woman, lineal indeed
From Pyrrha's pebbles or old Adam's seed.

Thus gentle Lamia judged, and judged aright,
That Lycius could not love in half a fright,
So threw the goddess off, and won his heart
More pleasantly by playing woman's part,

With no more awe than what her beauty gave,
That, while it smote, still guaranteed to save.
Lycius to all made eloquent reply,
Marrying to every word a twin-born sigh:
And last, pointing to Corinth, ask'd her sweet,
If 'twas too far that night for her soft feet.
The way was short, for Lamia's eagerness
Made, by a spell, the triple league decrease
To a few paces; not at all surmised
By blinded Lycius, so in her comprised.
They pass'd the city gates, he knew not how,
So noiseless, and he never thought to know.

    As men talk in a dream, so Corinth all,
Throughout her palaces imperial,
And all her populous streets and temples lewd,
Mutter'd, like tempest in the distance brew'd,

To the wide-spreaded night above her towers.
Men, women, rich and poor, in the cool hours,
Shuffled their sandals o'er the pavement white,
Companion'd or alone, while many a light
Flared, here and there, from wealthy festivals,
And threw their moving shadows on the walls,
Or found them cluster'd in the corniced shade
Of some arch'd temple door, or dusky colonnade.

  Muffling his face, of greeting friends in fear,
Her fingers he press'd hard, as one came near
With curl'd gray beard, sharp eyes, and smooth bald crown,
Slow-stepp'd and robed in philosophic gown
Lycius shrank closer, as they met and past,
Into his mantle, adding wings to haste,
While hurried Lamia trembled: "Ah," said he,
"Why do you shudder, love, so ruefully?
Why does your tender palm dissolve in dew?"—
"I'm wearied," said fair Lamia "tell me who
Is that old man? I cannot bring to mind
His features—Lycius! wherefore did you blind
Yourself from his quick eyes?' Lycius replied,

" 'Tis Apollonius sage, my trusty guide
And good instructor; but to-night he seems
The ghost of folly haunting my sweet dreams."

While yet he spake, they had arrived before
A pillar'd porch, with lofty portal door,
Where hung a silver lamp, whose phosphor glow
Reflected in the slabbed steps below,
Mild as a star in water; for so new
And so unsullied was the marble's hue,
So through the crystal polish, liquid fine,
Ran the dark veins, that none but feet divine
Could e'er have touch'd there.   Sounds Æolian
Breathed from the hinges, as the ample span
Of the wide doors disclosed a place unknown
Some time to any, but those two alone,

And a few Persian mutes, who that same year
Were seen about the markets: none knew where
They could inhabit; the most curious
Were foil'd, who watch'd to trace them to their house:
And but the flitter-winged verse must tell,
For truth's sake, what woe afterwards befell,
'Twould humor many a heart to leave them thus,
Shut from the busy world of more incredulous.

Love in a hut, with water and a crust,
Is—Love, forgive us!—cinders, ashes, dust;
Love in a palace is perhaps at last
More grievous torment than a hermit's fast:—
That is a doubtful tale from faery land,
Hard for the non-elect to understand.
Had Lycius lived to hand his story down,
He might have given the moral a fresh frown,

Or clench'd it quite, but too short was their bliss
To breed distrust and hate, that make the soft voice hiss.
Besides, there, nightly, with terrific glare,
Love, jealous grown of so complete a pair,
Hover'd and buzz'd his wings, with fearful roar,
Above the lintel of their chamber door,
And down the passage cast a glow upon the floor

   For all this came a ruin   side by side
They were enthroned, in the even tide,
Upon a couch, near to a curtaining
Whose airy texture, from a golden string,
Floated into the room, and let appear
Unveil'd the summer heaven blue and clear,
Betwixt two marble shafts —there they reposed,
Where use had made it sweet, with eyelids closed,
Saving a tithe which love still open kept,
That they might see each other while they almost slept,
When from the slope side of a suburb hill,
Deafening the swallow's twitter, came a thrill
Of trumpets—Lycius started—the sounds fled,
But left a thought, a buzzing in his head

For the first time, since first he harbor'd in
That purple-lined palace of sweet sin,
His spirit pass'd beyond its golden bourn
Into the noisy world almost forsworn
The lady, ever watchful, penetrant,
Saw this with pain, so arguing a want
Of something more, more than her empery
Of joys, and she began to moan and sigh
Because he mused beyond her, knowing well
That but a moment's thought is passion's passing bell,
"Why do you sigh, fair creature?" whisper'd he
"Why do you think?" returned she tenderly
' You have deserted me, where am I now?
Not in your heart while care weighs on your brow ·
No, no, you have dismiss'd me, and I go
From your breast houseless ay, it must be so."
He answer'd, bending to her open eyes,
Where he was mirror'd small in paradise,

"My silver planet, both of eve and morn!
Why will you plead yourself so sad forlorn,
While I am striving how to fill my heart
With deeper crimson, and a double smart?
How to entangle, trammel up and snare
Your soul in mine, and labyrinth you there,
Like the hid scent in an unbudded rose?
Ay, a sweet kiss—you see your mighty woes.
My thoughts! shall I unveil them? Listen, then!
What mortal hath a prize, that other men
May be confounded and abash'd withal,
But lets it sometimes pace abroad majestical,
And triumph, as in thee I should rejoice
Amid the hoarse alarm of Corinth's voice?
Let my foes choke, and my friends shout afar,
While through the thronged streets your bridal car
Wheels round its dazzling spokes"—The lady's cheek
Trembled; she nothing said, but, pale and meek,
Arose and knelt before him, wept a rain
Of sorrows at his words, at last with pain
Beseeching him, the while his hand she wrung,
To change his purpose. He thereat was stung,

48

Perverse, with stronger fancy to reclaim
Her wild and timid nature to his aim;
Besides, for all his love, in self-despite,
Against his better self, he took delight
Luxurious in her sorrows, soft and new.
His passion, cruel grown, took on a hue
Fierce and sanguineous as 'twas possible
In one whose brow had no dark veins to swell.
Fine was the mitigated fury, like
Apollo's presence when in act to strike
The serpent—Ha, the serpent! certes, she
Was none. She burnt, she loved the tyranny,
And, all subdued, consented to the hour
When to the bridal he should lead his paramour.

Whispering in midnight silence, said the youth,
"Sure some sweet name thou hast, though, by my truth,
I have not ask'd it, ever thinking thee
Not mortal, but of heavenly progeny,
As still I do.   Hast any mortal name,
Fit appellation for this dazzling frame?
Or friends or kinsfolk on the citied earth,
To share our marriage feast and nuptial mirth?"
"I have no friends," said Lamia, "no, not one;
My presence in wide Corinth hardly known
My parents' bones are in their dusty urns
Sepulchred, where no kindled incense burns,
Seeing all their luckless race are dead, save me,
And I neglect the holy rite for thee
Even as you list invite your many guests,
But if, as now it seems, your vision rests
With any pleasure on me, do not bid
Old Apollonius—from him keep me hid."
Lycius, perplex'd at words so blind and blank,
Made close inquiry, from whose touch she shrank,
Feigning a sleep; and he to the dull shade
Of deep sleep in a moment was betray'd

It was the custom then to bring away
The bride from home at blushing shut of day,
Veil'd, in a chariot, heralded along
By strewn flowers, torches, and a marriage song,
With other pageants; but this fair unknown
Had not a friend.   So being left alone

(Lycius was gone to summon all his kin),
And knowing surely she could never win
His foolish heart from its mad pompousness,
She set herself high-thoughted, how to dress
The misery in fit magnificence
She did so, but 'tis doubtful how and whence
Came, and who were her subtle servitors
About the halls, and to and from the doors,
There was a noise of wings till in short space
The glowing banquet-room shone with wide-arched grace.
A haunting music, sole perhaps and lone
Supportress of the faery roof, made moan
Throughout, as fearful the whole charm might fade.
Fresh carved cedar, mimicking a glade
Of palm and plantain, met from either side,
High in the midst, in honor of the bride
Two palms and then two plantains, and so on,
From either side their stems branch'd one to one
All down the aisled place; and beneath all
There ran a stream of lamps straight on from wall to wall
So canopied, lay an untasted feast
Teeming with odors.   Lamia, regal drest,

Silently paced about, and as she went,
In pale contented sort of discontent,
Mission'd her viewless servants to enrich
The fretted splendor of each nook and niche.
Between the tree-stems, marbled plain at first,
Came jasper panels; then, anon, there burst
Forth creeping imagery of slighter trees,
And with the larger wove in small intricacies.
Approving all, she faded at self-will,

And shut the chamber up, close, hush'd and still,
Complete and ready for the revels rude,
When dreadful guests would come to spoil her solitude.

The day appear'd, and all the gossip rout.
O senseless Lycius! Madman! wherefore flout

The silent-blessing fate, warm cloister'd hours,
And show to common eyes these secret bowers?
The herd approach'd, each guest, with busy brain,
Arriving at the portal, gazed amain,
And enter'd marvelling, for they knew the street,
Remember'd it from childhood all complete
Without a gap, yet ne'er before had seen
That royal porch, that high-built fair demesne,
So in they hurried all, mazed, curious and keen·
Save one, who look'd thereon with eye severe,
And with calm-planted steps walk'd in austere,
'Twas Apollonius· something too he laugh'd,
As though some knotty problem, that had daft
His patient thought, had now begun to thaw,
And solve and melt —'twas just as he foresaw

He met within the murmurous vestibule
His young disciple " 'Tis no common rule,
Lycius," said he, "for uninvited guest
To force himself upon you, and infest
With an unbidden presence the bright throng
Of younger friends, yet must I do this wrong,

And you forgive me." Lycius blush'd, and led
The old man through the inner doors broad-spread,
With reconciling words and courteous mien
Turning into sweet milk the sophist's spleen.

Of wealthy lustre was the banquet-room.
Fill'd with pervading brilliance and perfume.
Before each lucid panel fuming stood
A censer fed with myrrh and spiced wood,

Each by a sacred tripod held aloft,
Whose slender feet wide-swerved upon the soft
Wool-woofed carpets fifty wreaths of smoke
From fifty censers their light voyage took
To the high roof, still mimick'd as they rose
Along the mirror'd walls by twin-clouds odorous
Twelve sphered tables, by silk seats insphered,
High as the level of a man's breast rear'd
On libbard's paws, upheld the heavy gold
Of cups and goblets, and the store thrice told
Of Ceres' horn, and, in huge vessels, wine
Came from the gloomy tun with merry shine
Thus loaded with a feast the tables stood,
Each shrining in the midst the image of a God
When in an antechamber every guest
Had felt the cold full sponge to pleasure press'd,
By minist'ring slaves, upon his hands and feet,
And fragrant oils with ceremony meet
Pour'd on his hair, they all moved to the feast
In white robes, and themselves in order placed
Around the silken couches, wondering
Whence all this mighty cost and blaze of wealth could spring.

Soft went the music the soft air along,
While fluent Greek a vowell'd under-song
Kept up among the guests, discoursing low
At first, for scarcely was the wine at flow;
But when the happy vintage touch'd their brains,
Louder they talk, and louder come the strains
Of powerful instruments —the gorgeous dyes,
The space, the splendor of the draperies,
The roof of awful richness, nectarous cheer,
Beautiful slaves, and Lamia's self, appear,
Now, when the wine has done its rosy deed,
And every soul from human trammels freed,
No more so strange, for merry wine, sweet wine,
Will make Elysian shades not too fair, too divine
Soon was God Bacchus at meridian height,
Flush'd were their cheeks, and bright eyes double bright:
Garlands of every green, and every scent,
From vales deflower'd, or forest-trees branch-rent,
In baskets of bright osier'd gold were brought
High as the handles heap'd, to suit the thought
Of every guest; that each, as he did please
Might fancy-fit his brows, silk-pillow'd at his ease

What wreath for Lamia?　What for Lycius?
What for the sage, old Apollonius?
Upon her aching forehead be there hung
The leaves of willow and of adder's tongue;
And for the youth, quick, let us strip for him
The thyrsus, that his watching eyes may swim
Into forgetfulness; and, for the sage,
Let spear-grass and the spiteful thistle wage
War on his temples.　Do not all charms fly
At the mere touch of cold philosophy?
There was an awful rainbow once in heaven:
We know her woof, her texture; she is given
In the dull catalogue of common things.
Philosophy will clip an Angel's wings,
Conquer all mysteries by rule and line,
Empty the haunted air, and gnomed mine—
Unweave a rainbow, as it erewhile made
The tender-person'd Lamia melt into a shade.

By her glad Lycius sitting, in chief place,
Scarce saw in all the room another face,
Till, checking his love-trance, a cup he took
Full brimm'd, and opposite sent forth a look
'Cross the broad table, to beseech a glance
From his old teacher's wrinkled countenance,
And pledge him.   The bald-head philosopher
Had fix'd his eye, without a twinkle or a stir.

Full on the alarmed beauty of the bride,
Browbeating her fair form, and troubling her sweet pride.
Lycius then press'd her hand, with devout touch,
As pale it lay upon the rosy couch .
'Twas icy, and the cold ran through his veins ;
Then sudden it grew hot, and all the pains
Of an unnatural heat shot to his heart
"Lamia, what means this ?   Wherefore dost thou start ?
Know'st thou that man ?"   Poor Lamia answer'd not
He gazed into her eyes, and not a jot
Own'd they the lovelorn piteous appeal ·
More, more he gazed his human senses reel :
Some hungry spell that loveliness absorbs ,
There was no recognition in those orbs
"Lamia !" he cried—and no soft-toned reply.
The many heard, and the loud revelry
Grew hush · the stately music no more breathes ,
The myrtle sicken'd in a thousand wreaths
By faint degrees, voice, lute, and pleasure ceased ,
A deadly silence step by step increased,
Until it seem'd a horrid presence there,
And not a man but felt the terror in his hair

"Lamia!" he shriek'd, and nothing but the shriek
With its sad echo did the silence break
"Begone, foul dream!" he cried gazing again
In the bride's face, where now no azure vein
Wander'd on fair-spaced temples, no soft bloom
Misted the cheek, no passion to illume
The deep-recessed vision —all was blight,
Lamia, no longer fair, there sat a deadly white
"Shut, shut those juggling eyes, thou ruthless man!
Turn them aside, wretch! or the righteous ban
Of all the Gods, whose dreadful images
Here represent their shadowy presences,
May pierce them on the sudden with the thorn
Of painful blindness, leaving thee forlorn,
In trembling dotage to the feeblest fright
Of conscience, for their long-offended might,
For all thine impious proud-heart sophistries,
Unlawful magic, and enticing lies
Corinthians! look upon that gray-beard wretch!
Mark how, possess'd, his lashless eyelids stretch
Around his demon eyes! Corinthians, see!
My sweet bride withers at their potency"

"Fool!" said the sophist, in an under-tone
Gruff with contempt; which a death-nighing moan
From Lycius answer'd, as, heart-struck and lost,
He sank supine beside the aching ghost.
"Fool! fool!" repeated he, while his eyes still
Relented not, nor moved; "from every ill
Of life have I preserved thee to this day,
And shall I see thee made a serpent's prey?"
Then Lamia breathed death-breath; the sophist's eye,
Like a sharp spear, went through her utterly,
Keen, cruel, perceant, stinging: she, as well
As her weak hand could any meaning tell,
Motion'd him to be silent; vainly so;
He look'd and look'd again a level—No!
"A serpent!" echoed he; no sooner said,
Than, with a frightful scream, she vanished:
And Lycius' arms were empty of delight,
As were his limbs of life, from that same night.

On the high couch he lay!—his friends came round—
Supported him—no pulse or breath they found,
And in its marriage robe the heavy body wound.

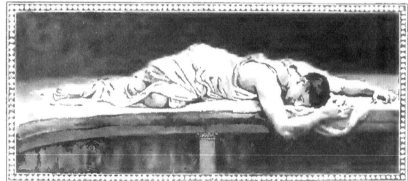

"Philostratus, in his fourth book *de Vita Apollonii*, hath a memorable instance in this kind, which I may not omit, of one Menippus Lycius, a young man twenty-five years of age, that, going betwixt Cenchreas and Corinth, met such a phantasm in the habit of a fair gentlewoman, which, taking him by the hand, carried him home to her house, in the suburbs of Corinth, and told him she was a Phœnician by birth, and if he would tarry with her, he should hear her sing and play, and drink such wine as never any drank, and no man should molest him, but she, being fair and lovely, would live and die with him, that was fair and lovely to behold. The young man, a philosopher, otherwise staid and discreet, able to moderate his passions, though not this of love, tarried with her awhile to his great content, and at last married her, to whose wedding, amongst other guests, came Apollonius, who, by some probable conjectures, found her out to be a serpent, a lamia, and that all her furniture was, like Tantalus' gold, described by Homer, no substance, but mere illusions. When she saw herself descried, she wept, and desired Apollonius to be silent, but he would not be moved, and thereupon she, plate, house, and all that was in it, vanished in an instant; many thousands took notice of this fact, for it was done in the midst of Greece."—BURTON's *Anatomy of Melancholy*, Part 3, Sect. 2, Memb. I Subs. I

LAMIA·WAS·WRITTEN·BY·JOHN·KEATS·WINCHEST[ER]·[·]ENGLAND·1819·THE·

DESIGNS·FOR·THE·POEM·WERE·DRAWN·BY· [·]·WILL·H·LOW·NEW·YORK·

AND·WERE·REPRODVCED·BY·

THE·FORBES·COMPANY·BOST[ON]

THE·TEXT·WAS·PRINTED·AND·

THE·BOOK·IS·PVBLISHED·BY·J·B·LIPPINCOTT·COMPANY·PHILADELPHIA·1888·

Lightning Source UK Ltd.
Milton Keynes UK
UKHW022317060922
408450UK00003B/32